Hanna-Barbera's
THE GREATEST ADVENTURE
STORIES FROM THE BIBLE

SAMSON AND DELILAH

text by
Christine L. Benagh

Based on a script by Harvey Bullock

ABINGDON PRESS
Nashville

Two young friends, Derek and Margo, are taking part in a ver[y] important dig in the Middle East. It is the opportunity of a lifetime for them to accompany her father, an archaeologist, on this expedition.

Most days their young nomad friend Moki, who is very curious about these things, joins them to as[k] a hundred questions and to keep things generally lively.

One especially hot and tiring day, the three friends are digging in their assigned spot, when the sand suddenly begins to give way. "Quic[k] sand," shouts Moki as the three

SAMSON AND DELILAH

ISBN 0-687-15745-5

MANUFACTURED BY THE PARTHENON PRESS AT NASHVILLE, TENNESSEE, UNITED STATES OF AMERICA

spiral down, down, down in a funnel of
sand.

Then just as unexpectedly the air is clear,
and they are in an enormous room. What a
spectacle! It is filled with treasure of every
sort—vases, jars, statues, jewelry and
ornaments, pillars, furniture of gold and
ivory.

"How magnificent," whispers Derek in
awe.

"Wow," murmurs Moki.

Margo has moved ahead of the others
toward a huge bronze door. The latch
fastening the two massive panels is a
golden scarab beetle. She puts her hand on
the scarab, translating its message: *All who
enter here go back in time.* Suddenly, the
great doors swing open into what appears
to be a cavern of light.

"Come on," she calls, and without
hesitation the others follow.

They step over the threshold and —

Once they stepped through the door, they were in darkness. But they were not alone; they heard rustlings close by.

"I wish I hadn't come," whispered Moki. "There is somebody out there."

"Don't worry." Derek patted his shoulder. "It's probably just crickets." The words were hardly out of his mouth when there came a deep, bone-chilling roar.

"That's not crickets," Moki gasped. "That's a lion, and there are probably bears and snakes and crocodiles—"

Margo prodded him along. "Just keep moving."

They stumbled through the darkness, with Moki working hard to keep himself between Margo and Derek. Faint flickers of light appeared on the horizon.

"That has to be a town," Derek said. "We'll be safe there."

A sturdy stone wall surrounded the town, and two soldiers guarded the closed gates. One of them lowered his spear and shouted, "Who goes there?"

"Travelers," replied Derek. "We're looking for a safe place to spend the night."

"Lions are chasing us!" Moki's tone was urgent. "There are hundreds of them."

"These gates stay shut." The second man, an officer, approached them. "We have a lion cornered inside the town."

The soldier laughed. "Actually it's Samson, a worthless Israelite who has been troubling us for years. But we have him now. He's inside the locked gates and cannot get out."

The officer peered in through the slot. "Here he comes. The guards have him trapped!" He turned and shoved Derek out of the way.

Inside a handsome giant of a man came striding toward the gate, his thick black hair streaming out behind. He took scant notice when four Philistine soldiers leaped out of the shadows. Shouts and groans were heard.

"They have him! They have him!" The officer pounded the ground with his spear.

But the noise came from the four attackers, whom Samson had brushed aside like mosquitoes. He continued down the street without breaking his stride and came crashing through the heavy gates as if they were not there. Pausing just long enough to lift one gate onto his back, he disappeared into the night.

Moki turned to the astonished guards. "So much for having him trapped."

The three travelers followed Samson into the night. "I think we'll be safe with *him*," said Moki.

They waited until morning to approach the big man. The first light showed him sleeping peacefully in a grassy spot with the gate serving as his pillow.

"Good morning," Margo ventured.

Samson was awake in an instant and on his feet.

Moki pointed to the gate. "We would have knocked, but it was already open."

Derek had taken a loaf of bread out of his backpack. He held it out. "Have some breakfast."

Samson smiled, took the loaf in his enormous hands, and tore off a piece. "Where did you three come from?"

"We followed you from the city last night," Margo explained as she took a piece of the bread.

Samson tossed his flowing locks. "Those murderous Philistines. They will stop at nothing to kill me."

"But why?" asked Derek.

"Because they are cruel people. They have overrun the whole land of Israel. They take our grain, our grapes—all our crops—murder innocent families, and destroy our towns."

"You sure destroyed them last night," put in Moki.

"I do what I can, but I am only one man," Samson shook his head sadly, "the only Israelite who will stand up to them."

"With your enormous strength, there may be hope." Margo indicated the gate lying on the ground.

"There is always hope," Samson agreed, "but is it enough? I'll set this here as a reminder to my people that we must continue our fight against these Philistines who have taken away our freedom." He lifted the gate and shoved it into the ground as if it were a garden stake. "I must be on my way. Would you like to come along?"

As they approached the Israelite town of Zorah, a young boy went running down the street crying, "Samson's coming! Samson's coming!" People appeared in doorways, leaned out windows, or gathered at the edge of the road to greet him, and Samson had a wave and a smile for each one as he passed.

The boy, meanwhile, had come running back and fell in beside Samson, taking giant steps.

Moki found himself pushed aside.

"Who are you?" the boy asked him angrily.

"A friend of Samson's," Moki bragged. "We took care of some Philistines last night. Who are you?"

"My name is Micah." The boy raised his fists. "So you're a fighter. Let's see how good you are."

Moki didn't like the looks of this. He turned expecting to find Samson beside him, but his new friend had continued on his way. Moki ran after him as fast as he could go.

Beside the roadway an ox and cart were mired in the mud, and an old man tried vainly to free them. Samson placed himself in front of the ox and took a grip on the horns. One mighty tug had the animal and cart back on the road. A roar of approval came from the townspeople. Samson took a bow and continued on his way.

M argo, Derek, and Moki followed Samson into a quiet courtyard garden where the temple stood. The priest came out to meet the hero. "We are all pleased to see you again."

"It is good to be back," Samson smiled. "But you know I will not be here long. I cannot stay cramped in the town. I plan to return to my cave in Etam as soon as I collect some provisions."

"Samson, that is not wise." The priest put a hand on the great arm. "The Philistines know about your hideout, and they will be watching for you."

"Don't worry," Samson laughed. "Let them find me. They will be the sorry ones."

He turned to Moki. "Come, little friend, let me show the view from the temple roof. You can see for miles across our beautiful land."

Derek and Margo stayed in the courtyard with the priest.

"What a man!" exclaimed Derek.

"I've never seen anyone so strong," added Margo.

"Nor one so reckless." The priest looked worried. "Samson is a great man in Israel. He is generous and loyal, gentle with his friends and ruthless with his enemies. His strength cannot be matched.

"The people love to tell of the time he went to visit a beautiful girl in Timnath. The way led through some of our wildest country, and in a rock pass a huge lion sprang on him. Any other man would have been dead in an instant, but Samson ripped the furious beast apart as if it had been a lamb."

"He must be indestructible," Derek remarked.

"Not quite." The priest looked at them solemnly. "It is true that Samson is the hope of our people, but he is human—a man with two serious weak spots."

"I don't understand," said Margo.

"He has never been able to resist a beautiful woman," the priest continued, "and this has got him into dangerous situations many times. His great strength is a special gift from God, but it will last only so long as he keeps a solemn, secret vow."

The priest lowered his voice. "If his enemies were to discover the secret, they could remove his strength from him completely. I only pray that our God will protect him." He turned and went into the temple.

Margo turned to Derek. "What in the world could he mean by that?"

Samson's cave retreat was high on a craggy hillside. A spring of clear water gurgled over the rocks nearby. "What more could one want?" Samson surveyed the scene. "There is cool shelter, game for the taking, everything." A huge boulder covered the cave entrance, and Samson rolled it aside as if it had hinges.

For their part, Margo, Derek, and Moki were trying to recover their breath after the steep climb.

"Samson," someone called. A stooped, cowering man came hesitantly from behind a crag.

"Welcome, Zebel," Samson greeted him. "Come meet my friends."

Zebel took no notice. He went slowly toward Samson, never lifting his eyes off the ground. "Why did you come here?" he quavered. "The Philistines have followed you. Come look." He led them to the other side of the hill.

In the valley below was a large encampment of soldiers. The smoke from their cooking fires clouded the morning air.

Zebel was wringing his hands. "You only bring us trouble. Don't you realize that they rule the land?"

"They do not," Samson snapped. "We are Israelites, men of Judah, we must not let them rule over us."

"But we are too weak," Zebel whined. "Why do you antagonize them?"

"I want to make them uncomfortable here, and I only do to them what they do to me." Samson looked out once more at the Philistine camp. "Step aside, Zebel, I will go down and confront them myself. This is not your problem."

"Wait, Samson," squeaked the little man, "this time it *is* our problem."

Samson stared. "What do you mean?"

Zebel's voice was so low they could hardly hear him. "The Philistines have—have threatened us. They will kill us and our wives and children with us, unless—unless we deliver you into their hands, bound so that you cannot escape. Please, Samson, don't let us die."

Samson looked at Zebel. There was scorn in his voice, "They have chosen a foul way to capture me. But you are right. I do not want you to perish. You may bind me."

Two men carrying lengths of strong new rope crept out from behind the rocks where they had been hiding. They dared not look at Samson as they went about their work.

Margo, Derek, and Moki watched in stunned silence. Then Derek whispered,

"We must get back to the priest and let him know what is happening."

"Hurry," Moki pleaded.

They took off at top speed.

Trembling, Zebel led the heavily bound Israelite to the captain of the Philistines. "Hmm-m," the officer tugged and tested the ropes. "They are tight enough." He turned to Zebel, "You may go now that you have done your dirty work."

"So," the captain addressed his prisoner, "your own people betray you." Samson said nothing.

"And now," his tormentor sneered, "we are going to take you to Gaza so that all our people can enjoy your execution."

Several soldiers surrounded Samson and began pulling him along by the rope around his neck. The road followed a winding way through a scorched and barren waste. The sun beat mercilessly on the procession.

The captain rode just ahead of Samson and was talking to a fellow officer. "This means the end of all resistance in Israel. With Samson out of the way we can make quick work of the rest of the people."

"Yes," replied his companion. "It will mean the end of the nation and of their false god."

At this Samson snapped upright and stopped in his tracks. The veins in his temples began to bulge as he strained against his bonds. The pressure of those muscles burst the ropes like twine. The

soldier nearest to Samson made a grab, but one blow from the huge hand sent him sprawling.

The column of soldiers stopped. Close beside the track lay the carcass of a donkey, bleached by the sun. Samson picked up the jawbone and held it threateningly in front of him.

"Charge," bellowed the captain. "What are you waiting for? He has only a bone for a weapon."

The soldiers were circling around Samson and started to close in. He wielded the jawbone like a scythe and mowed down row after row as they came on.

The captain rode in behind Samson with his sword raised. A quick backhand blow sent him tumbling from his horse. The desert sand was littered with soldiers.

When Moki and the others dashed into the temple courtyard, they found Micah playing with a wooden sword.

"Get the priest. Get the priest," shouted Derek. "Quick."

The priest had already heard the commotion. "What is it?"

"It's Samson!" Margo gasped for breath. "Samson—Samson is . . ."

"Did someone call me?" They all looked to see the giant coming into the courtyard. He was a bit rumpled, but smiling.

"What happened?" asked Moki.

Samson held up his weapon. "With the jawbone of a donkey, I have made donkeys of the Philistines."

With a mighty throw, Samson sent the bone sailing right over the temple. "Come with me, friends. This calls for a celebration." He left the courtyard with Moki and Micah running to keep up.

Margo turned to bid the priest good-bye. "They certainly do not know the secret of his strength yet."

"We must pray that they never will," he replied. "Go along with him now and take care."

Samson's house was plain but comfortable, and it provided the travelers with a chance to do their laundry.

Derek sat in the shade changing the laces in his shoes. Moki was rinsing out clothes, while Margo hung them to dry.

"What a waste of time." Moki squeezed the last piece. "We'll only get these things dirty again."

Samson emerged from the house with a pack on his back. "The place to celebrate is not here, my friends," he said. "We are going to the Sorek Valley and spend a couple of days in the most beautiful place in the world."

"Sounds great." Derek got up eagerly and came to join the others, but he tripped over Moki's laundry bucket. Samson rushed to help him to his feet.

"Ouch!" Derek winced as he put his foot on the ground.

Margo looked wistfully at Samson. "We won't be able to go. Derek has sprained his ankle."

"Don't be silly," Derek laughed. "You go ahead. I don't mind staying behind. I can use the rest."

Samson led Margo and Moki through the pleasant valley country and into a bustling town. The Philistines who lived there seemed to melt away as the party made its way along the main street to a handsome sprawling house. The woman standing in the open doorway was very lovely. Samson's face lighted when he saw her. "Delilah," he called.

"Samson," she cried in delight. "What a surprise!"

"I've brought two friends. This is Margo and Moki."

"Welcome to my house. Come in, the door is open. You won't have to tear this one off its hinges." She laughed softly and patted Samson's arm as he led the others inside.

She turned to follow them, when a

hooded figure darted from behind the corner of the house and beckoned to her. A troubled look passed over Delilah's smooth brow, and she bit her lip nervously. At last she nodded and called inside, "Make yourselves comfortable. I will be right back."

Then she followed the dark figure down the street, looking back over her shoulder again and again.

Delilah's house was not only elegant, it had everything to make one comfortable. Moki sighed with pleasure as he sank into the deep cushions on an ivory couch. Samson disappeared into the back rooms. "I'll see if I can find some refreshment," he called.

"This is the life for me," Moki said. "Samson sure knows how to pick 'em. Delilah is a knockout."

Margo went on looking at the luxurious furnishings without saying a word. "Well, isn't she?" pressed Moki.

"Yes—" Margo paused and then added, "but something is not right here. Where did she get all this? What is she doing out there in the town? The people here are Samson's enemies, you know."

Samson's enemies were at that moment talking to Delilah. The shrouded messenger had led her through a low doorway on a nearby side street where the lords of the Philistines were plotting. Included in the group was the army captain, whose face carried the scar inflicted by the donkey's jawbone.

The spokesman for the group approached her. "We can never capture Samson by force. All of us together are no match for him."

"I know that all too well," said the captain, touching his wound.

The leader continued, "We know there must be some secret to his great strength. We must find out what it is, and for that we need your help."

"Oh no," Delilah objected. "I will have no part in murder."

Another noble interrupted, "Of course not, my dear, we would not ask you to do such a thing. We do not intend to kill Samson. We want him very much alive."

"It would be a good object lesson for the Israelites," the chief conspirator continued. "You would be doing your people a great service."

Delilah hesitated ever so slightly. "But Samson is my dear friend. The answer is no."

"Does he bring gifts worthy of you?" asked one of the men. "Does he bring jewels and perfumes and silks?"

"Well, no, but . . ."

"This will!" The leader sprang forward holding a gold coin between his fingers.

Delilah's eyes widened, but at last she said, "No, it would not be right. Samson is my good friend."

"A gold coin can be a better friend," the man continued. "Think what you could do if you had many of them."

There was a long pause. "How many?" she asked finally.

"Eleven hundred." He held the coin so that it glittered in the sunlight coming through the doorway. "From each of us," added the captain.

Delilah's lips twitched and a faint smile spread over them as she held out her hand. Her fingers closed eagerly over the coin he placed in it. She nodded and left the room.

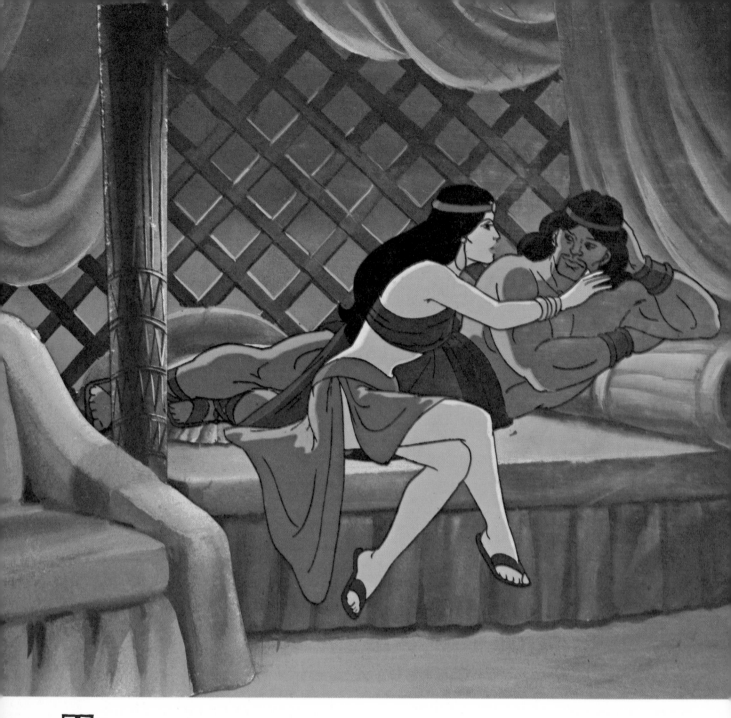

That evening after Margo and Moki were asleep, Delilah crept softly to where Samson lay. She caressed his forehead, and he opened his eyes. "I'm glad you are here," she whispered. "Samson, I want to ask you a question."

"Yes, I love you," he murmured sleepily.

"And I love you," she purred, "but that is not the question."

"Yes, you are the only woman for me."

Samson's eyes closed again, and his head drooped.

"Samson," she breathed close to his ear, "you are so wonderfully strong. What is the secret of your great strength? I am dying to know."

Samson opened one eye, cocked his head, and looked at her.

"I'm just curious." She brushed his hand with a kiss.

He closed his eyes again. "Well," he mumbled drowsily, "if you were to bind me with seven green willow switches, I would be helpless." Minutes later he was snoring loudly.

Next evening as soon as Samson was asleep, Delilah approached his couch. The Philistines had brought her the green willow, and when she had him firmly bound, she slipped to a draped doorway. "Be ready. I am going to wake him."

"Samson," she cried, "the Philistines are upon you."

The sleeper jumped to his feet and the willow switches fell from him like so much paper.

"Why, you lied to me!" screeched Delilah. She turned and stamped out of the room.

Within a couple of days Derek's ankle had mended, and he had also become good friends with the priest. They were sitting together on the roof of the temple. "I think I can join my friends now," Derek said. "They have gone to Sorek with Samson."

"What!" exclaimed the priest. "That means he is with Delilah, the deceitful one. I have a terrible premonition. You must get to him at once and warn him not to break his vow. He is in grave danger as long as he is with that woman."

"What is the vow? And the secret?" asked Derek.

"It is a very strange story," the old man began. "Some years ago Manoah and his wife lived in this very village. They were a very pious couple, and they wanted children badly. But they had none.

"One day as the wife was working in a field, an angel of the Lord appeared to her and told her she would have a child, a son. But the angel also told her that the boy would be a Nazarite from the day of his birth until he died."

"What's a Nazarite?"

"Someone who is dedicated to God at birth. The man who is a Nazarite has made a vow never to drink wine or to let a razor touch his head."

"So that's why he has such long hair," said Derek.

"If it is ever cut, his strength will desert him. If anyone can get his secret out of him, it is Delilah. You are young and swift, hurry to him

with this ring. It will remind him of his vow."

The priest stood up and pointed toward a line of hills in the east. "It is only a few miles in that direction."

They went down into the courtyard, and there in front of the temple door stood a party of Philistine soldiers. "We have come to collect our tax," said the leader.

"What is the meaning of this?" the priest spoke sharply. "You will surely hear from Samson when he finds out."

The soldier laughed. "Samson is only one man. Besides, he is not going to find out because no one leaves here without paying the tax."

As they turned back into the temple Derek brushed against a long silken drape. "I have an idea." He turned to the priest, "Could you let me have some of this silk?"

"Why yes."

"It will need to be sewed," Derek went on.

"Miriam, a woman of the village is very good with a needle. I am sure she will help you."

"And I'll need some willow branches."

"We have those in the courtyard," said the priest. "You must have a plan."

"I do," said Derek. "And one more thing, we must pray for wind. I am going to fly right over the Philistines."

During the following day Delilah refused to speak to Samson.

"I'm sorry I teased you," he pleaded. There was no reply.

Delilah filled a bowl with fruit and swept past Samson. He followed along behind.

When she got to the temple, she approached the towering statue of the god Dagon. She set the bowl in front of the idol and stood looking up.

"I thought you were teasing me," Samson attempted.

Delilah spoke without looking at him. "If you loved me you would share your secret."

Margo and Moki had also tagged along and had stopped behind a pillar to wait. They heard the word "secret."

"Oh no," whispered Margo. "This is terrible."

Samson went on trying to appease Delilah. "I made a promise." She did not respond. "If you will speak to me, I will tell you," said the unhappy man.

Delilah turned and smiled at him. "Will you swear before Dagon that you are not lying to me?"

"I will have nothing to do with your god. I am a Nazarite, a man of God."

"Well, go on, tell me," urged Delilah.

Samson leaned over and whispered in her ear.

Moki grabbed Margo's arm. "Things really look bad."

"I know," she agreed. "I'm truly frightened."

Later that night Delilah stepped into a small side room where six Philistine soldiers were hiding. "He has told me the secret of his strength. I have bound him with new ropes, and they will leave him powerless. Wait for my signal."

She returned to the sleeping Samson and shouted, "Wake up, Samson, the Philistines are upon you."

He sprang from the couch and the ropes dropped to the floor.

Delilah covered her face with her hands and began to sob. Samson looked at her bewildered.

Next morning he approached his lady in the garden. "Delilah, why don't we spend a pleasant day together. We could take a boat and go down the river, and—"

"Take someone you trust," she snapped.

"I came here to be with you. You know how I feel about you."

"That's just it," she tossed her head, "I don't."

Moki had been watching this scene from a window. He turned to Margo. "Good news, Delilah is talking to Samson today."

"That may not be good at all. She is probably still trying to wangle his secret out of him. I don't understand why he is not suspicious."

"You may be worrying too much," said Moki. "Samson is smart."

"He's also in love," Margo pointed out.

Moki looked puzzled. "Can't you be both?"

"Please, Delilah," Samson was begging. "Come out for a boat ride today, and tonight I will tell you the secret. It has something to do with my hair."

She brightened, "Your hair?"

"Yes, truly, but I'm hoping to make you forget all about it."

"I probably will forget," she lied.

The day's outing tired everyone except the watchful Delilah. As soon as she was sure Samson was asleep, she tiptoed to his side and moved her weaving loom close. He did not stir.

She went to the room where the Philistines waited. "Be ready. This time I have the secret. You must give me time to weave the seven braids of his hair into my loom."

"Samson," she cried, "the Philistines are upon you."

He leaped to his feet and felt the loom holding his hair. He yanked out the pin and smashed the frame to splinters. His strength was as great as it had always been.

Delilah was furious. "You have lied to me again. Why do you mock me?"

Samson was also angry. "Because I do not think this should be important between us."

"Then nothing can be important between us." Delilah's sharp reply was interrupted by a scuffling sound from the next room.

"Someone is in there," said Samson. "What is going on here?"

Just for a moment there was panic in the woman's eyes, but then she recovered herself. "Why don't you look for yourself? I'm probably hiding Philistine soldiers in there to destroy you."

"Oh Delilah," he muttered, "I didn't say that."

"My dear Samson," Delilah poked her slender finger into his brawny chest. "Either you trust me, or you must leave in the morning."

At the temple in Zorah, Derek had hardly stopped to rest or eat. He cut large pieces of bright silk curtain and showed Miriam how to sew them together and to make narrow casings or tunnels on the outer edges. Then he peeled the willow branches and ran them through the casings.

The priest looked on as Derek lifted his homemade hang glider. "Do I understand that you are planning to fly right over the soldiers?"

"Is that possible?" asked Miriam.

"We'll find out tomorrow," Derek replied.

"Take this ring and give it to Samson," said the priest. "He'll know he's in danger."

As Derek was leaving, the priest said almost to himself, "I only hope that Samson can keep his secret until you get there."

The next morning dawned bright in Zorah. Derek, Miriam, and the priest were on the roof. Outside were the unsuspecting soldiers.

The priest cautioned Derek, "Perhaps you should delay. There are so many Philistines."

"I need all the time I can get," Derek said. He was arranging the bright silk wings on either side and grasping the sling. "I'll be over them before they know what is happening." He backed to the farthest edge of the roof and began to run. With a leap he launched himself onto the flowing air.

The glider dipped low and out of sight of the watchers. "He will be killed," said the priest. But then the glider rose into view, the brilliant wings billowing.

"What was that?" asked the officer below.

"I didn't see anything, sir," responded the soldier beside him.

"It was a shadow of some sort," said the captain. "Not a cloud—there is not a one in the sky."

"Probably a big bird," offered the soldier.

Derek saw a canyon opening in front of him and headed for the sheer cliffs where there would be updrafts. As he

flew deeper into the canyon, the air became more turbulent, and his little craft was tossed about violently. One sharp updraft sent him soaring, and then a sudden downdraft plunged him toward the canyon floor. He struggled and strained to keep the glider in balance, leaning first to the left and then to the right, as he dipped and dropped. He was only a few feet from the jagged rocks when he managed to get things under control and swing up and away. But not before the right wing had hit the ground and ripped a corner.

From here on it was a struggle. The wind kept tearing at the ruptured wing tip. The glider was harder and harder to control, but Derek could see the town ahead. "Steady, steady," he kept saying. All the while the rip kept lengthening.

Finally he had to bring his craft down in a tree for a crash landing. The bright sails settled into the branches, and he grasped one limb and held on tight. After surveying the scene he let go, and dropped to the

ground. Nothing was broken, so he dusted himself off and headed for Sorek. By the time he got there night had fallen. He asked directions to Delilah's house.

Delilah had spent her day charming Samson, and he was so relieved to be in her good graces that he paid little attention to her questions about the source of his strength.

Once he was asleep she came softly into the room and knelt beside him. Stroking his head, she whispered into his ear. "Remember, dear, you have promised to tell me this secret of yours."

He roused slightly. "I—I'm a-a Nazarite, and I have promised God . . . that . . ."

"That what?" she persisted.

"That—that no razor will—ever touch my head."

She sensed at once that this was the truth. She sat close by stroking his hair until he was fast asleep again. Then she summoned a soldier to bring a razor.

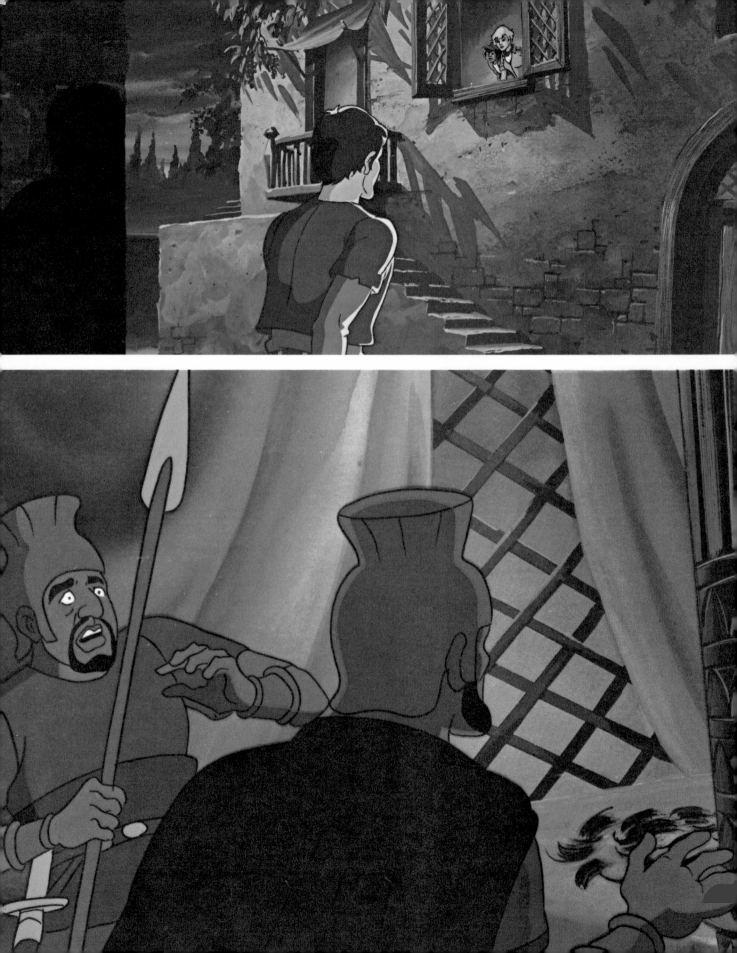

Margo and Moki were too worried to sleep. They leaned out of a window looking at the moonlit street and talking about the day's events.

"Delilah has him wrapped around her finger," said Moki.

"I do not see how we can stop her," Margo sighed.

Moki straightened and pointed. "Look, here comes Derek!"

Derek saw them waving and came to the window. "Is Samson there? Let me in quickly."

He was barely inside when they heard the cry. "Wake up, Samson, the Philistines are upon you!"

"Too late," groaned Derek. They headed in the direction of the sound. The scene made Margo burst into sobs.

Samson had risen from his bed to confront six armed Philistines. His proud head was bald, the luxurious black locks were strewn over his pillow. He clenched his fists and made for his enemies, but the small hand of Delilah stopped him. He had not even the strength to break her hold.

He turned to her in horror. "You have betrayed me. O God, forgive me."

The soldiers led the helpless giant out of the room.

Moki moaned softly, "Can't we help him?"

"There is nothing we can do," Derek replied. "There is nothing anyone can do." He led his friends away from the heartbreaking scene.

The Philistine captain returned and poured a shower of gold coins into Delilah's outstretched hands. She stood as if in a trance. Tears ran down her cheeks, and the coins ran through her fingers to the floor.

It was a long time before Derek and Margo and Moki chanced to get to Zorah again, but Derek always thought they might. He still had the priest's ring and wanted to give it back.

"We are here to return your ring," he said as the priest came to greet them.

"Please tell us what happened to Samson," Margo begged.

"We have never forgotten him," Moki added.

"Samson's end was as amazing as his beginning," said the priest. He motioned for them to sit down. "The Philistines put out his eyes and chained him to a great millstone to grind their grain.

"But his vow as a Nazarite was for life, and without his enemies' noticing it, his hair grew again and his strength returned with it.

"On one of their festival days, the people were reveling in the temple of Dagon, pouring wine before the idol and making merry. They decided to make sport of their famous prisoner. The soldiers brought the humbled champion and placed his hands against two great pillars of the temple, and the people began to mock and tease him.

"Samson just stood silently with head bowed, but he was praying: 'O Lord God, remember me, I pray thee, and strengthen me, I pray thee, only this once, O God. . . . Let me die with the Philistines.'

"And he bent down and pressed against the pillars with all his might. The stones cracked, and the whole building crumbled and fell. The idol of Dagon came crashing down with the rest.

"Samson died with the Philistines, but in his death he killed more of them than he had done in life."

Then his brothers and his father's
whole family went down to get him.
They brought him back and buried him
between Zorah and Eshtaol in the tomb
of Manoah his father. He had led Israel
for twenty years.

Oh Almighty God I hope you will forgive me from all my sins I try to do my best and I know I can't be perfect.

a men